Copyright, 1904
by
Adèle Millicent Smith

Printed by
The John C. Winston Co.
Philadelphia

Exercises in Proofreading

BY

Adèle Millicent Smith

Exercise I

READING Copy

The Reader's occupation is sedentery in the extreme, and the monotynous hum of his own or the Copyholders voice is apt to induce a drowsy condition in which the most palpable blunders may escape notice. One of the most dedly traps of the inexperenced is the easily contracted habit of reading mechanicaly, without atending to the sence while it justaseasy to err in the other way, and by reading solely for sense, to be blind to litteral erors of grave importance. As the result of long experience, I find that I am rarely chalenged as to matter about which I have had doubts. it is the false security induced by Oblivion and day-dreaming that is priductive of heart-searching references to copy.

The International Printer.

The copy should be read aloud to the correcter by some personwhocan pronounce distintly and with ease every word contained in it. The correcter holds the proof and the Reader the copy. Corcection should be made on the black margin, opposite the lines in which the erors are respectively found, and in ezactly the same order in which the errors occur. Corections are generally seperated from each other by oblique lines. When severel errors occur in one line, the changes shuold bemadeon the margen nearest the several errors wich they are intended to corect.

Copyright, 1904,
by
Adèle Millicent Smith

Printed by
The John C. Winston Co.
Philadelphia

Exercises in Proofreading
by
Adèle Millicent Smith

BLOCK-PRINTING

Printing from engraved blocks of wood on soft metal was practised in the fourteenth century when rude figures of the Virgen and other Saints, often coarsely colored by hand, made their appearance About the same time ornamental paterns were printed on stuff from engraved blocks. Cardboards was developed jrom paper, and playing-cards, printed from blocks, were common in the forteenth and fifteenth centures. All these methods of printing were so many decided advanced toward typography. but two new proceses still were necssary to success, viz: a thicker ink than previoulyused, and some kind of a press with wich to make a regular and even impresion.

The next step was making of that interest class of books called "block-books. There consisted for the most part of a *series* of rude woodcuts the full size of the pages representing various parts of Scripture, Histry,heaven, Hell, death, and the Jubgment. The earliest known specimens of those works were printed in a brown ink similar to distemper drawings. Lamp black was already well known to the anceints as a bases for writing ink, and mixed with gum water, formed that deep glozy hue so much admired in many old manuscripts but how to thicken the ink as to make it suitable for printing, from a raised surface was a discovry of great importance, made long before topography was invented. This object was atained by the prolonged boiling of oil and then grinding it with carbon of lampblack.

The Pentateuch of Printing: Blades.

Copyright, 1904
by
Adèle Millicent Smith

Printed by
The John C. Winston Co.
Philadelphia

EXERCISES IN PROOFREADING
BY
ADÈLE MILLICENT SMITH

EXERCISE III

THE POINT SYSTEM

Formerly the varous sizes of type were made somewhat hap. hazard; the name given to the different sizes as Pica, primer, brevier, bourgois, nonpareil not always conforming to the exact measurements which the severel names were supposedtoindicate Twenty years ago, in 1883 the United Typefounders association adapted the American Point System, now universaly used in this country. The system established the *point*, one-twelfth of pica size, as the unit of measurement, and all siZes are multiples of this unit pearl, 5 point; nonpareil, 6; minion 7; brevier, 8 bourgeois, 9. Each type bears a simple definite pro portion to all others and cannot be used in combinations therewith. This Point system involves a charge in types styles, and the designer had not only to be acquainted with the inovation, but also had to understand what it signifid, to no where it limited his scope, and were, on the other hand, it gave him wider fredom. The adaptation of the American systems and other improvements made thereby posible has placed typefounding in this couutry on a more scientific bases, and tHe designers have been corespondingly required to adjust thier art to more scientific lines

JOHN V. SEARS, in THE INTERNATIONAL
PRINTER; "MODERN TYPE FORMS.

Copyright 1904,
by
Adèle Millicent Smith

Printed by
The John C. Winston Co
Philadelphia

Exercise IV

MANUSCRIPT BOOKS

The manscript books of the Middle ages were vertable works of art. Time was of no consquence to the copyist, and many years were often employed intheproduction of a simple book. The works of the manuscript writers consist in outlining the letter for the text, first drawing in the letters and afterwards filling them in with the pen. The style of lettering usully adapted by the copyist is preserved in a form modified in the _Old English_ and german text letters used by modren printers and in the ecleciastical lettering used for inscriptions in churches. When the copyist had completed his work the manuscript was taken in hand by the designer, who skeched in the initial letter, ornamental borders, and pictures and handed it over to the iluminator, who painted in the colouring. The design and iluminating seem to have been really the most important feature in some of these early books and many splendid manuscripts, with there elabrate initials and delicate flourishes and tracry spreading over the entire margins, are in existence still, reminders of an Art that existed once but now has passed away, perhaps forever.

Ernest J. Hathaway, in The International Printer, "The Influence of Religion in Early Bookmaking."

Copyright, 1904,
by
Adèle Millicent Smith

Printed by
The John C. Winston Co.
Philadelphia

EXERCISES IN PROOFREADING
BY
ADÈLE MILLICENT SMITH

EXERCISE V

EARLY PRINTING-PRESSES

The fisrt printer had but small presses, made entirely
of wood. There power also was slight and they printed
as a rule, but one page a time. the screw was of wood,
and worked by a bar,'' much thesameas a modren napkin
press. The chiefthing was to obtain an even surface on
the "bed" upon wnich the page of type rest; and seo-
ondly, an even surtace for the "Platen," whicц was lowered as the bar tur nedthe screw, and thus pressed the
paper upon the face of the type. The eveness of impres
sion, as well as colour in many old books, show that this
was acomplished with grate success, and proʌes what
good mecanicians they were fore hundred years ago.

It is a task whih we could not accomplish so successfully where our modern tools and apliances withdrawn

* * * * * * * * * * * * * * *

There was nearly always two workmen to one press. One
"beat" the "Form," that is he dabbed two big soft balls
covered with ink all over the type; the other placeg the
white paper on the "tympan, and ran the hole, by means
of a whinch, beneath the *platen*, and then made a strong
pull at the bar.

THE PENTATEUCH OF Printing: Blades

Copyright, 1904,
by
Adèle Millicent Smith

Printed by
The John C. Winston Co.
Philadelphia

Exercises in Proofreading
BY
Adèle Millicent Smith

Exercise VI

NEWSPAPER PRINTING

The paper from which news-papers are printed ⅌ ω·· made in very long webs or rolls, varʃing in length from ℊ three to ninety miles, and prepared at special mills. A roll of paper is pla ced at one end of the press above the flour. and the end of the sheet is then led between the cylinders. The paper which enters the press simply as a

blank roll, flies swiftly from cilinder to cylinder, receiting the impression of streotypes, electrctypes, and half-tones separates in newspapers uuder the action of the knife, divides again into sections, and issues form the press in the form of the finished newspaper, nearly tolded and counted ready for delivery.

The first Journal in America apeared in Boston on September 25th, 1690, under the name Public Occurences This was a pamphlet, rather than a newspaper. The Boston *News-Letter* was started in 1704. The Boston Gazette appeared on December 21 1719, and the American Weekly Mercury, of Philedelphia, one day later. The Pennsylvania-*Gazette* of philadelphia was started in 1728 by Samuel Kiemer, but in less then a year it was baught by Benjamin Frankli . In 1821, it took the name of *The* Saturday Evening *Post;* under this title it is still issued and is the *oldest* existing Journal in America.

Copyright, 1904,
by
Adèle Millicent Smith

Printed by
The John C. Winston Co.
Philadelphia

EXERCISES IN PROOFREADING
BY
ADÈLE MILLICENT SMITH

EXERCISE VII

THE INVENTION OF TYPOGRAPHY

The key to the invention of Typography was the typemould.   The honor is dne to the men who invented the f irst type-mold, for types which are *cast* are the ones only that can be used to advantage. A fierce controvercy has waged as to who first gave the world a knowlege of topography, but the wieght of evidence is strongly in favor of John Gutenberg, a printer of mainz We do not know when or were Guttenberg made his 1st experiments with movable type, but before 1459 he seems at Strasburg to have been at work, endeavoring to prefect his art. From Strasbourg he went to MainZ where his name appeared in 1448 in a record of a legal contract. Here about 1450, he enters into partner-ship with Johann means necesary to set up a printing-press.
FustorFaust, a wealthy moneylender, who furnished the
In a few years (1445), Fust brought a law suit against Gutenburg to recover of the sum money he had advanced. Yhe verdict was in Fusts favor, and as Guttenberg could not pay the money, the printingpress passed out of his harʹds. Although now nearly old, sixty years Gutunberg did not dispair, but determined to find another berg did not dispair, but determined to find another office. Some of his printing still materials remained to him, and the Clerk of the town of Mainz provided him with mony. He continued to work for some time in Mainz. His death occurred about 1448.

Copyright, 1904,
by
Adèle Millicent Smith

Printed by
The John C. Winston Co.
Philadelphia

EXERCISES IN PROOFREADING
BY
ADÈLE MILLICENT SMITH

EXERCISE VIII

EARLIEST PRINTED Works

The earlest specimen of printing from mov able metal
types known to exist at the present day is the famour
Letter of Indulgence, of pope Nicholas V, to persons such
as should contribute money to help the King of Cyprus
against the Turʒs.   A copy of this Indulgenoe now
preserved at the Hage, bears the earliest date authentic
on a document printed from type November 15, 1454.

The work upon which Gutenburg's fame rests as a
a graet printer is the holy Bible in Latin.   There are
are ʒ editions of this work one known as the Bible of
Forty two Lines and the otʏer as the Bible of *Thirty-six*
Lines.

It is known not was which printed first, but it is is
generally beleived that the the forty-two line Bible is
earlier.   It is beleved that this Bible could have been
begun before August 1450, and that it was finished in
1453, but the exact dates are not known. These 2
editions of the Bible bears no printed date.   The first
book with a printed date is the Psalmorum codex of 1457,
isued by Schœffer.   This Palter *Codex* is regarded by
many as the finest works issued by the early press.
It is an imtation not only of the copyists but of the iluminators art, with block stately types, and two colored
initials red and blue.

Copyright, 1904,
by
Adèle Millicent Smith

Printed by
The John C. Winston Co.
Philadelphia

Exercise IX

MODERN PRESSWORK

In comparing the press-work of the sixteenth century with that of the close of the 19th, it would be satisfaction if we could not point to the same proßress in the *quality* of work that we find in speed with which the work is excuted. Unfortunately it must be admited that that this is not uniformly the case. Not little satisfactory bookprinting is produced by the modern press; but nevertheless it is the case that the demands made now upon the printer for books whichcanbesold at a poplar price has a tendenoy to bring fourth a quantity of press-work for which it is not posible to express admiration. It is with a feeling of great relief that one turns from some of the grey pages of the present ful old black-letter volumes of two or 3 centuries sinse, day, printed u*p*on hard and stiff pulp paper, to the delight-with their clearcut sharp type, struck wih deep black ink on hand-made paper, of such stock as admited not only on a perfect impression, but in addition, presented a surface and a flexibility delightful to the eye and to to the the touch.

Authors and Publishers: G. H. P. and J. B. P.

The numorous illustrations which gives life and add value to our books, magazines and news-papers, without their increasing greatly cost, have been brought in existence by the developement of the relatively new art of Photo-engraving, which by 1880, was beginning to suppliant the reproducing of woodcuts.

Reproductions of any picture or obJect in which there is a gradtion of color, is made by the half-tone process. Drawings or hictures consisting of single lines, that is without tones of color are produced by lineplates.

Copyright, 1904,
by
Adèle Millicent Smith

Printed by
The John C. Winston Co.
Philadelphia

EXERCISES IN PROOFREADING
BY
ADÈLE MILLICENT SMITH

EXERCISE X

THE ROMAN AND the ITALIC TYPES

In 1458, the King of France sent Nicholas Jenson to Mianz to learn the new art   On his retuın to Paris he tried to get sufficient mony to establish the press, but was not sucessful and went to Italy   In Venice, he became famous. Jonsen prefected the roman type, whicb he used in 1471. but the latter had allready been cast at Subaco in 1465. The roman letter of Jonson was a letter of extra ordinary beauty, it has freqently been copied, but never imitated. Our roman letter of to-day is deried from the two scripts formally used in Romecapitals from the letters used from insriptions, and small letters form the kursive form employed for busness cor respondence.

Aldus manutius was an eminent printer; who lived in Venece at the begining of the sizteenth century. He he desired a compact type for the purpOse of issuing small editions of the classies, and to supply this need he introduced the type first knon as Venitian but called italic afterward by the Latin and the English people. It is a a letter wich inclines to the right, and is suppoed to be formed from the hand-writing of Petrarch. The aldine press established at Venice was celehrated for its cditions of the greek and and Latin classies. To assist him in the prepration of these volumes, Aldos gathered around him, editors and and proof-readers, the most scolarly men of his age. The present system of Punctuation may be said have been devized by him, as but few marks before his time had been emploqed, and the use of those was not well-regulated

Copyright, 1904,
by
Adèle Millicent Smith

Printed by
The John C. Winston Co.
Philadelphia

EXERCISES IN PROOFREADING
BY
ADÈLE MILLICENT SMITH

EXERCISE XI

THE GOTHIC LETTER

The book issued by the first printers were in the Gothic characters. When the new art was introduced first the wealthy looked upon the inovation as an artistic trade, and the printers copied therefore the characters of of the cotemporary manuscript in order to sell there works. The gothic letters had been emplyoed by the ccpyists of Europe for many centuries before the invenvention of movable types Roman type was first cast in 1465 by two German printers, Sweinhem and Panartz at Subiaco, Italy. It was afterward prefected and used by Nicholas Jensen, at Venice, The gothic and the Roman froms strugled together for some time after the interduction of printing but the letter finally triumpfed. Roman type was used first in England in 1818, and by by the year 1800 books were printed generally in in that type. The roman letter of Jonson was the modle adopted by William Morris for the Kelmacott press, when it was started at Hammersmith England, in 1891

Although in printed work gothic characters   proceded the roman, the letter had been emplo∕ed in manuscript many centuries before the introduction of gothic letters.   Gothic letter in fact was formed from the roman.

The English name of *black letter* was given to the caracacter until after the introduction of roman printing types. Old English and German text are callcd by printers black letters.

Copyright, 1904,
by
Adèle Millicent Smith

Printed by
The John C. Winston Co.
Philadelphia

EXERCISES IN PROOFREADING
BY
ADÈLE MILLICENT SMITH

EXERCISE XII

WILLIAM CAXTION

William Caxton is the first printer who practiced the Art in England. The Aear of his burth is not definitely known; but it it was probably near 1422, for he was aprenticed in 1438 to the mercers trade A few years after the latter date he left England for the low Countries where he remained for 30 years. About 1470, he entered the service of Margret, Duchess uf Burgundy and sister of Edward IV. Caxtion had long been intrested in the romances of the days and had translated some them. Having finished and been rewarded for his trouble in translating Le Recueil des Histoires de Troyes for the duchess of Burgundy, he found his books in great demand. The English Nobles at Bruges whished to have copies of the favorite romances of the Age, and Caxton found himself able to supply the demahd with suficient rapidty. This brings us to the year 1472, or 1473 Mansoin who had obtained some knowlege of art of printing, although certainly not from Colone, had just begun his topographical labors at Brugs, and was ready to reproduce copies by means of the press, if supported by the necesary patronage and funds. Caxton found the money, and Madsion the requisite knowledge, by the aid of wich appeared "The Recuyell," the book first printed in the english language. This, probably was notaccomplished till 1474, and was succeeded on Caxtons part, in another yea, by an issue of the Chess Book.

Copyright, 1904,
by
Adèle Millicent Smith

Printed by
The John C. Winston Co.
Philadelphia

EXERCISES IN PROOFREADING
BY
ADÈLE MILLICENT SMITH

EXERCISE XIII

PRINTING IN CHINA and JAPAN

In China, various attempts have been made to substute type for engraved blocks, but this is difficult because of the great numbers of the Chinese Characters. These caracters do net stand for letters, or sounds, but represent complete words, or ideas the characters formed by combination have been variously estimated, from 40 thousand to over two-hundred-thousand in numbers; not more than forteen or fifteen thousand, however, are in reglar use. A c hinese Missionary house employs about six thonsand characters for an ordinary news-paper; only about four thousand are neccessary; while magazines which treat of a great range of subjects requires ten thousand. The printing offices arrange the characters by the radicles. Moʌable types both of wood and of metel, have been employed long in China. Printing from movabel metal types are practised in China mainly for the pur pose of cir culating the Bible and the news-papers.

It is indisputable, that block-printing was first practiced in China, but there is nothing which prove that Europe origibally dirived her knowledge of this art   from the east.

In Japan, the earliest example of block printing dates from the midle of the eight century .Because of the avidity with which the Japanese have took hold of western learning, printing is extensively carried on on Japan, both blocks, and types of metal being employed.

Copyright, 1904,
by
Adèle Millicent Smith

Printed by
The John C. Winston Co.
Philadelphia

EXERCISES IN PROOFREADING
BY
Adèle Millicent Smith

EXERCISE XIV

BEGINNING OF PRINTING IN AMERICA.

In America, printing begun in the City of Mexico. The first printer was Juana Pablos, and the first book printed was La Escala Espiritual para Llegar al Cielo" (A Spiritual Ladder for Reaching Heaven of San Juan Climaco, isued about 1636. So so far as known, no copy of this book exists now. A press was established at Lima Peru, about 1584. The first printing press in North America was ereoted at Cambridge, Massachusets, through the efforts of the Rev. Joss or Jessie Glover, who died while bringing the matcrials to that place. Glovers wife married Henry Dunster the President of Harvard Ccllege, and he resumed the management of the Press. It was opperated by Stephen Day, a workmen who sailed with Glover, in 1639 it it issued "The Freeman's Oath" and an almanac. Its first important work was was The Bay Psam Book," printed in 1640

Printing was begun in 1676 in Boston by John Foster. The first press in Philadelphie was set by William Bradford and the first work issued by him was an almanic in 1685. Bradford afterward moved to New York and begun printing in that oity city in 1693.

Among the early books published in America, a few still retain there interest, for only not their quaintness but because of the influence they have exerted on the national character.

John Cotton's Catechism, or "Mlik for Babies," first issued in England, was reprinted at Cambridge, Massachussetts, in 1656. This Catechism was afterwards included in another famuus book, "The New England Premer," the first edetion of which is supposed to have appeared, between 1687 and 1690. The only feature which must have made the Primer poplar with children was its illustrations, especialy the rymed alphabet cuts. █

Copyright, 1904,
by
Adèle Millicent Smith

Printed by
The John C. Winston Co.
Philadelphia

Exercises in Proofreading
BY
Adèle Millicent Smith

Exercise XV

BENJAMIN FRANKLIN

Benjamin Franklin was born in Boston on the 17 of
of January, 1706, and died in Philadelphla, on the 17th of April
1790. He begun his apprenteceship as a printer in 1778, and
worked as a journey-man in Philedelphia in 1724, and in in London
worked as a journey-man in Philedelphia in 1724, and in in London
in 1725. He returned to Philadelphia in 1726, and soon began
as master brinter in 1729. As editor and publisher he there made
him self a man of note. He vented the Franklin stove in 1742,
he proved the identity of lighting and eleotricity in 1752 he
was made Clerk of the Assembly in 1736; post-master of Philadel-
representative of Pensylvania before the Ccuncil of Engalnd in
1757 and again in 1764; deleegate to congress in 1775; ambassader
to France in 1770; commissioner to England in 1783; President
of Pennsylvania from 1785 to 1787; delegate from the Constitutional
Convention in 1789.

THE PRACTICE OF TYPOGRAPHY:
Theodore Low DeVinne

In 1732, Franklin issued the first numbers of "Poor Richards
Almanac," which was pubblished every year, for a quarter of a
a eentury. "Poor Richard" made Franklin famous. He had
had notioed that in many hcmes this almanic was the only book.
He therefor filled the space between the remarkeble days in
the calander with proverbal sentences, inculcating industry and
frugality as the means of obtaining wealth and therebye according
to Franklins belief) securing virtue; for he though that the
way to make people happy was to help them to be good.
To the counsels of Poor Richard are due to some extent
the shrewd, industrous and thrifty habits of the typical American'

Exercises in Proofreading
BY
Adèle Millicent Smith

Copy—I

READING COPY

The reader's occupation is sedentary in the extreme, and the monotonous hum of his own or of the copyholder's voice is apt to induce a drowsy condition in which the most palpable blunders may escape notice. One of the most deadly traps of the inexperienced is the easily contracted habit of reading mechanically, without attending to the sense; while it is just as easy to err in the other way, and, by reading solely for sense, to be blind to literal errors of grave importance. As the result of long experience, I find that I am rarely challenged as to any matter about which I have had doubts. It is the false security induced by oblivion and day-dreaming that is productive of heart-searching references to copy.

THE INTERNATIONAL PRINTER.

The copy should be read aloud to the corrector by some person who can pronounce distinctly and with ease every word contained in it. The corrector holds the proof and the reader the copy. Corrections should be made on the blank margins, opposite the lines in which the errors are respectively found, and in exactly the same order in which the errors occur. Corrections are generally separated from each other by oblique lines. When several errors occur in one line, the changes should be made on the margin nearest the several errors which they are intended to correct.

Printed by
The John C. Winston Co.
Philadelphia

Exercises in Proofreading
BY
Adèle Millicent Smith

Copy—II

BLOCK-PRINTING

Printing from engraved blocks of wood or soft metal was practised in the fourteenth century, when rude figures of the Virgin and other saints, often coarsely coloured by hand, made their appearance. About the same time ornamental patterns were printed on stuffs from engraved blocks. Cardboard was developed from paper, and playing-cards, printed from blocks, were common in the fourteenth and fifteenth centuries. All these methods of printing were so many decided advances toward Typography; but two new processes were still necessary to success, viz: a thicker ink than previously used, and some kind of press with which to make a regular and even impression.

The next step was the making of that interesting class of books called "block-books." These consisted for the most part of a series of rude woodcuts the full size of the page, representing various parts of Scripture, History, Heaven, Hell, Death, and the Judgment. The earliest known specimens of these works were printed in a brown ink similar to distemper drawings. Lampblack was already well known to the ancients as a basis for writing ink, and, mixed with gum water, formed that deep glossy hue so much admired in many old manuscripts; but how to thicken the ink so as to make it suitable for printing from a raised surface was a discovery of great importance, made long before typography was invented. This object was attained by the prolonged boiling of oil, and then grinding it with carbon or lampblack.

The Pentateuch of Printing: *Blades.*

Printed by
The John C. Winston Co.
Philadelphia

Exercises in Proofreading
by
Adèle Millicent Smith

Copy—III

THE POINT SYSTEM

Formerly, the various sizes of type were made somewhat haphazard; the names given to the different sizes, as pica, primer, brevier, bourgeois, nonpareil, not always conforming to the exact measurement which the several names were supposed to indicate. Twenty years ago, in 1883, the United Typefounders Association adopted the American point system, now universally used in this country. This system establishes the point, one-twelfth pica size, as the unit of measurement, and all sizes are multiples of this unit: pearl, 5-point; nonpareil, 6; minion, 7; brevier, 8; bourgeois, 9. Each type bears a simple, definite proportion to all others and can be used in combination therewith. This point system involved a change in type styles, and the designer not only had to be acquainted with the innovation, but had also to understand what it signified, to know where it limited his scope, and where, on the other hand, it gave him wider freedom. The adoption of the American system and other improvements thereby made possible have placed typefounding in this country on a more scientific basis, and the designers have been correspondingly required to adjust their art to more scientific lines.

John V. Sears, in The International Printer: "Modern Type Forms."

Printed by
The John C. Winston Co.
Philadelphia

Exercises in Proofreading
BY
Adèle Millicent Smith

Copy—IV

MANUSCRIPT BOOKS

The manuscript books of the middle ages were veritable works of art. Time was of no consequence to the copyist, and many years were often employed in the production of a single book. The work of the manuscript writers consisted in outlining the letter for the text, first drawing in the letters and afterward filling them in with the pen. The style of lettering usually adopted by the copyists is preserved in a modified form in the Old English and German text letters used by modern printers, and in the ecclesiastical lettering used for inscriptions in churches.

When the copyist had completed his work the manuscript was taken in hand by the designer, who sketched in the initial letters, ornamental borders, and pictures, and handed it over to the illuminator, who painted in the coloring. The designing and illuminating seem to have been the most important features in some of these early books; and many splendid manuscripts, with their elaborate initials and delicate flourishes and tracery spreading over the entire margins, are still in existence, reminders of an art that once existed but has now passed away, perhaps forever.

Ernest J. Hathaway, in The International Printer: "The Influence of Religion in Early Bookmaking."

Printed by
The John C. Winston Co,
Philadelphia

Exercises in Proofreading
BY
Adèle Millicent Smith

Copy—V

EARLY PRINTING-PRESSES

The first printers had but small presses made entirely of wood. Their power also was slight and they printed, as a rule, but one page at a time. The screw was of wood, and worked by a "bar," much the same as a modern napkin press. The chief thing was to obtain an even surface on the "bed" upon which the page of type rested; and, secondly, an even surface for the "platen," which was lowered as the bar turned the screw, and thus pressed the paper upon the face of the type. The evenness of impression, as well as of colour, in many old books, shows that this was accomplished with great success, and proves what good mechanicians they were four hundred years ago. It is a task which we could not now accomplish so successfully were our modern tools and appliances withdrawn.

* * * * * * * * * * * * * * * * *

There were nearly always two workmen to one press. One "beat" the "form," that is, he dabbed two big soft balls covered with ink over all the type; the other placed the white paper on the "tympan," and ran the whole, by means of a winch, beneath the platen, and then made a strong "pull" at the bar.

THE PENTATEUCH OF PRINTING: *Blades.*

Printed by
The John C. Winston Co.
Philadelphia

EXERCISES IN PROOFREADING
BY
ADÈLE MILLICENT SMITH

COPY—VI

NEWSPAPER PRINTING

The paper from which newspapers are printed is made in long webs or rolls, varying in length from three to nine miles, and is prepared at special mills. A roll of paper is placed at one end of the press just above the floor, and the end of the sheet is led between the cylinders. The paper, which enters the press simply as a blank roll, flies swiftly from cylinder to cylinder, receiving the impressions of stereotypes, electrotypes, and half-tones, separates into newspapers under the action of the knife, again divides into sections, and issues from the press in the form of the finished newspaper, neatly folded and counted, ready for delivery.

The first journal in America appeared in Boston on September 25th, 1690, under the name of Publick Occurrences. This was a pamphlet rather than a newspaper. The Boston News-Letter was started in 1704. The Boston Gazette appeared on December 21st, 1719, and The American Weekly Mercury of Philadelphia one day later. The Pennsylvania Gazette of Philadelphia was started in 1728 by Samuel Keimer, but in less than a year it was bought by Benjamin Franklin. In 1821 it took the name of The Saturday Evening Post; under this title it is still issued, and is the oldest existing journal in America.

Printed by
The John C. Winston Co.
Philadelphia

EXERCISES IN PROOFREADING
BY
Adèle Millicent Smith

Copy—VII

THE INVENTION OF TYPOGRAPHY

The key to the invention of typography was the type-mould. The honor is due to the man who invented the first type-mould, for types which are cast are the only ones that can be used to advantage. A fierce controversy has waged as to who first gave to the world a knowledge of typography, but the weight of evidence is strongly in favor of John Gutenberg, a printer of Mainz.

We do not know when or where Gutenberg made his first experiments with movable types, but before 1439 he seems to have been at work at Strasburg, endeavoring to perfect his art. From Strasburg he went to Mainz, where his name appears in 1448, in a record of a legal contract. Here, about 1450, he entered into partnership with Johann Fust, or Faust, a wealthy money-lender, who furnished the means necessary to set up a printing-press. In a few years (1455), Fust brought a lawsuit against Gutenberg, to recover the sum of money he had advanced. The verdict was in Fust's favor, and as Gutenberg could not pay the money, the printing-press passed out of his hands. Although now nearly sixty years old, Gutenberg did not despair, but determined to found another office. Some of his printing materials still remained to him, and the clerk of the town of Mainz provided him with money. He continued to work for some time in Mainz. His death occurred about 1468.

Printed by
The John C. Winston Co.
Philadelphia

EXERCISES IN PROOFREADING

BY

ADÈLE MILLICENT SMITH

COPY—VIII

EARLIEST PRINTED WORKS

The earliest specimen of printing from movable metal types known to exist at the present day is the famous Letter of Indulgence, of Pope Nicholas V, to such persons as should contribute money to help the King of Cyprus against the Turks. A copy of this Indulgence, now preserved at the Hague, bears the earliest authentic date on a document printed from types—November 15th, 1454.

The work upon which Gutenberg's fame rests as a great printer is the Holy Bible in Latin. There are two editions of this work: one known as the Bible of Forty-two Lines and the other as the Bible of Thirty-six Lines. It is not known which was printed first, but it is generally believed that the forty-two-line Bible is the earlier. It is believed that this Bible could not have been begun before August, 1450, and that it was finished in 1455, but the exact dates are not known. These two editions of the Bible bear no printed date. The first book with a *printed* date is the Psalmorum Codex of 1457, issued by Schoeffer. This Psalter is regarded by many as the finest work issued by the early press. It is an imitation not only of the copyist's but of the illuminator's art, with black stately types, and two-colored initials, red and blue,

Copy—IX

MODERN PRESSWORK

In comparing the presswork of the sixteenth century with that of the close of the nineteenth, it would be a satisfaction if we could point to the same progress in the quality of work that we find in the speed with which this work is executed.   Unfortunately, it must be admitted that this is not uniformly the case.   Not a little satisfactory book-printing is produced by the modern press, but it is nevertheless the case that the demands made upon the printer now for books which can be sold at a popular price have a tendency to bring forth a quality of presswork for which it is not always possible to express admiration.

It is with a feeling of relief that one turns from some of the gray and muddy pages of the present day, printed upon hard and stiff "pulp" paper, to the delightful old black-letter volumes of two or three centuries since, with their clear-cut sharp type, struck with deep black ink on hand-made paper of such stock as admitted not only of a perfect impression, but, in addition, presented a surface and a flexibility delightful to the eye and to the touch.

AUTHORS AND PUBLISHERS: G. H. P. AND J. B. P.

The numerous illustrations which give life and add value to our books, magazines, and newspapers, without greatly increasing their cost, have been brought into existence by the development of the relatively new art of photo-engraving, which by 1880 was beginning to supplant the reproducing of woodcuts.

Reproductions of any picture or object in which there is a gradation of color, are made by the half-tone process. Drawings or pictures consisting of simple lines, that is without tones of color, are reproduced by line-plates.

Printed by
The John C. Winston Co.
Philadelphia

Exercises in Proofreading

BY

Adèle Millicent Smith

Copy—X

THE ROMAN AND THE ITALIC TYPES

In 1458 the King of France sent Nicolas Jenson to Mainz to learn the new art. On his return to Paris he tried to get sufficient money to establish a press, but was not successful and went to Italy. In Venice he became famous. Jenson perfected the roman type, which he used in 1471, but the letter had already been cast at Subiaco in 1465. The roman type of Jenson was a letter of extraordinary beauty; it has frequently been copied, but never equaled. Our roman letter of to-day is derived from the two scripts formerly used in Rome—capitals from the letters used for inscriptions, and small letters from the cursive form employed for business correspondence.

Aldus Manutius was an eminent printer who lived in Venice at the beginning of the sixteenth century. He desired a compact type for the purpose of issuing small editions of the classics, and to supply this need he introduced the type first known as Venetian but afterward called italic by the Latin and the English peoples. It is a letter which inclines to the right, and is supposed to be formed from the handwriting of Petrarch.

The Aldine press established at Venice was celebrated for its editions of the Greek and Latin classics. To assist in the preparation of these volumes, Aldus gathered around him, as editors and proofreaders, the most scholarly men of the age. The present system of punctuation may be said to have been devised by him, as before his time but few marks had been employed, and the use of these was not well regulated.

Printed by
The John C. Winston Co.
Philadelphia

EXERCISES IN PROOFREADING
BY
Adèle Millicent Smith

Copy—XI

THE GOTHIC LETTER

The books issued by the early printers were in the gothic character. When the new art was first introduced, the wealthy looked upon the innovation as an inartistic trade, and the printers therefore copied the characters of the contemporary manuscripts in order to sell their works. The gothic letter had been employed by the copyists of Europe for several centuries before the invention of movable types. Roman type was first cast in 1465 by two German printers, Sweinheym and Pannartz, at Subiaco, Italy. It was afterward perfected and used by Nicolas Jenson, at Venice. The gothic and the roman forms struggled together for some time after the introduction of printing, but the latter finally triumphed. Roman type was first used in England in 1518, and by the year 1600, books were generally printed in that character. The roman letter of Jenson was the model adopted by William Morris for the Kelmscott Press, when it was started at Hammersmith, England, in 1891.

Although in printed works the gothic character preceded the roman, the latter had been employed in manuscripts many centuries before the introduction of the gothic letter. Gothic letter, in fact, was formed on the roman.

The English name of black letter was not given to the gothic character until after the introduction of roman printing-types. Old English and German Text are called by printers black letter.

Printed by
The John C. Winston Co.
Philadelphia

Exercises in Proofreading
BY
Adèle Millicent Smith

Copy—XII

WILLIAM CAXTON

William Caxton is the first printer who practised the art in England. The year of his birth is not definitely known, but it was probably near 1422, as he was apprenticed in 1438 to the mercer's trade. A few years after the latter date, he left England for the Low Countries, where he remained for thirty years. About 1470 he entered the service of Margaret, Duchess of Burgundy and sister of Edward IV. Caxton had long been interested in the romances of the day and had translated some of them. Having finished and been rewarded for his trouble in translating "Le Recueil des Histories de Troyes" for the Duchesss of Burgundy, he found his book in great request. The English nobles at Bruges wished to have copies of this the favorite romance of the age, and Caxton found himself unable to supply the demand with sufficient rapidity. This brings us to the year 1472 or 1473. Colard Mansion, who had obtained some knowledge of the art of printing, although certainly not from Cologne, had just begun his typographical labours at Bruges, and was ready to produce copies by means of the press, if supported by the necessary patronage and funds. Caxton found the money, and Mansion the requisite knowledge, by the aid of which appeared "The Recuyell," the first book printed in the English language. This, probably, was not accomplished till 1474, and was succeeded, on Caxton's part, in another year, by an issue of the "Chess Book."

Printed by
The John C. Winston Co.
Philadelphia

EXERCISES IN PROOFREADING
BY
Adèle Millicent Smith

Copy—XIII

PRINTING IN CHINA AND JAPAN

In China various attempts have been made to substitute types for engraved blocks, but this is difficult because of the great number of the Chinese characters. These characters do not stand for letters or sounds, but represent complete words or ideas; the characters formed by combinations have been variously estimated from forty thousand to over two hundred thousand in number; not more than fourteen or fifteen thousand, however, are in regular use. A Chinese missionary house employs about six thousand characters; for an ordinary newspaper only about four thousand are necessary; while magazines, which treat of a greater range of subjects, require ten thousand. The printing-offices arrange the characters by the radicals. Movable types, both of wood and of metal, have long been employed in China. Printing from movable metal types is practised in China mainly for the purpose of circulating the Bible and for newspapers.

It is indisputable that block-printing was first practised in China, but there is nothing to prove that Europe originally derived her knowledge of this art from the East.

In Japan the earliest example of block-printing dates from the middle of the eighth century. Because of the avidity with which the Japanese have taken hold of Western learning, printing is extensively carried on in Japan, both blocks and types of metal being employed.

Printed by
The John C. Winston Co.
Philadelphia

EXERCISES IN PROOFREADING
BY
ADÈLE MILLICENT SMITH

COPY—XIV

BEGINNINGS OF PRINTING IN AMERICA

In America printing began in the city of Mexico. The first printer was Juan Pablos, and the first book printed was "La Escala Espiritual para Llegar al Cielo" (A Spiritual Ladder for Reaching Heaven) of San Juan Cilmaco, issued about 1536. So far as known, no copy of this book now exists. A press was established at Lima, Peru, about 1584. The first printing-press in North America was erected at Cambridge, Massachusetts, through the efforts of the Rev. Joss or Jesse Glover, who died while bringing the materials to that place. Glover's wife married Henry Dunster, the president of Harvard College, and he assumed the management of the press. It was operated by Stephen Daye, a workman who sailed with Glover, and in 1639 it issued "The Freeman's Oath" and an almanac. Its first important work was the "The Bay Psalm Book," printed in 1640.

Printing was begun in Boston in 1676, by John Foster. The first press in Philadelphia was set up by William Bradford, and the first work issued by him was an almanac, in 1685. Bradford afterward removed to New York and began printing in that city in 1693.

Among the early books published in America, a few still retain their interest, not only for their quaintness but because of the influence they have exerted on the national character.

John Cotton's Catechism, or "Milk for Babes," first issued in England, was reprinted at Cambridge, Massachusetts, in 1656. This catechism was afterward included in another famous book, "The New England Primer," the first edition of which is supposed to have appeared between 1687 and 1690. The one feature which must have made the Primer popular with children was its illustrations, especially the rhymed alphabet cuts.

Printed by
The John C. Winston Co.
Philadelphia

Exercises in Proofreading
by
Adèle Millicent Smith

Copy—XV

BENJAMIN FRANKLIN

Benjamin Franklin was born in Boston on the 17th of January, 1706, and died in Philadelphia on the 17th of April, 1790. He began his apprenticeship as a printer in 1718, and worked as a journeyman in Philadelphia in 1724, and in London in 1725. He returned to Philadelphia in 1726, and there began as master printer in 1729. As editor and publisher he soon made himself a man of note. He invented the Franklin stove in 1742; he proved the identity of lightning and electricity in 1752; he was made clerk of the Assembly in 1736; postmaster of Philadelphia in 1737; deputy postmaster-general for the Colonies in 1753; representative of Pennsylvania before the Council of England in 1757, and again in 1764; delegate to Congress in 1775; ambassador to France in 1776; commissioner to England in 1783; president of Pennsylvania from 1785 to 1787; delegate to the Constitutional Convention in 1787.

The Practice of Typography:
Theodore Low DeVinne.

In 1732 Franklin issued the first number of "Poor Richard's Almanack," which was published every year for a quarter of a century. "Poor Richard" made Franklin famous. He had noticed that in many homes this almanac was the only book. He therefore filled the spaces between the remarkable days in the calendar with proverbial sentences inculcating industry and frugality as the means of obtaining wealth and thereby (according to Franklin's belief) securing virtue; for he thought that the way to make people good was to help them to be happy. To the counsels of Poor Richard are due to some extent the shrewd, industrious, and thrifty habits of the typical American.

Exercise I—Corrected

READING Copy

The Reader's occupation is sedentary in the extreme, and the monotonous hum of his own or the Copy-holders voice is apt to induce a drowsy condition in which the most palpable blunders may escape notice. One of the most deadly traps of the inexperienced is the easily contracted habit of reading mechanicaly, without atending to the sense, while it just as easy to err in the other way, and by reading solely for sense, to be blind to litteral errors of grave importance. As the result of long experience, I find that I am rarely chalenged as to matter about which I have had doubts. It is the false security induced by Oblivion and day-dreaming that is productive of heart-searching references to copy.

The International Printer.

The copy should be read aloud to the corrector by some person who can pronounce distintly and with ease every word contained in it. The corrector holds the proof and the Reader the copy. Correction should be made on the black margin, opposite the lines in which the errors are respectively found, and in exactly the same order in which the errors occur. Corections are generally seperated from each other by oblique lines, When several errors occur in one line, the changes should be made on the margin nearest the several errors wich they are intended to corect.

Copyright, 1904,
by
Adèle Millicent Smith

Printed by
The John C. Winston Co.
Philadelphia

EXERCISES IN PROOFREADING
BY
ADÈLE MILLICENT SMITH

EXERCISE II—CORRECTED

BLOCK-PRINTING

Printing from engraved blocks of wood or soft metal was practised in the fourteenth century, when rude figures of the Virgin and other Saints, often coarsely colored by hand, made their appearance. About the same time ornamental paterns were printed on stuff from engraved blocks. Cardboards was developed from paper, and playing-cards, printed from blocks, were common in the forteenth and fifteenth centuries. All these methods of printing were so many decided advanced toward typography, but two new proceses still were necssary to success, viz: a thicker ink than previouly used, and some kind of press with wich to make a regular and even impresion.

The next step was making of that interest class of books called "block-books. These consisted for the most part of a series of rude woodcuts the full size of the pages, representing various parts of Scripture, Histry, Heaven, Hell, death, and the Judgment. The earlest known specimens of those works were printed in a brown ink similar to distemper drawings. Lamp black was already well known to the ancients as a bases for writing ink, and mixed with gum water, formed that deep glosy hue so much admired in many old manuscripts but how to thicken the ink as to make it suitable for printing from a raised surface was a discovry of great importance, made long before typography was invented. This object was atained by the prolonged boiling of oil, and then grinding it with carbon of lampblack.

THE PENTATEUCH OF PRINTING: Blades.

Copyright, 1904,
by
Adèle Millicent Smith

Printed by
The John C. Winston Co.
Philadelphia

EXERCISES IN PROOFREADING
BY
ADÈLE MILLICENT SMITH

EXERCISE III—CORRECTED

THE POINT SYSTEM

Formerly the various sizes of type were made somewhat haphazard; the name given to the different sizes, as Pica, primer, brevier, bourgois, nonpareil not always conforming to the exact measurements which the several names were supposed to indicate. Twenty years ago, in 1883, the United Typefounders Association adapted the American Point System, now universaly used in this country. The system established the *point*, one-twelfth of pica size, as the unit of measurement, and all sizes are multiples of this unit pearl, 5 point; nonpareil, 6; minion, 7; brevier, 8 bourgeois, 9. Each type bears a simple, definite proportion to all others and cannot be used in combinations therewith. This Point system involves a change in types styles, and the designer had not only to be acquainted with the inovation, but also had to understand what it signifid, to no where it limited his scope and were, on the other hand, it gave him wider fredom. The adaptation of the American system and other improvements made thereby posible has placed typefounding in this couytry on a more scientific basis, and tHe designers have been corespondingly required to adjust their art to more scientific lines.

JOHN V. SEARS, IN THE INTERNATIONAL
PRINTER, "MODERN TYPE FORMS."

Copyright, 1904,
by
Adèle Millicent Smith

Printed by
The John C. Winston Co.
Philadelphia

EXERCISE IV—CORRECTED

MANUSCRIPT BOOKS

The manscript books of the Middle ages were veritable works of art. Time was of no consquence to the copiist, and many years were often employed in the production of a simple book. The works of the manuscript writers consist in outlining the letter for the text, first drawing in the letters and afterwards filling them in with the pen. The style of lettering usully adapted by the copyist is preserved in a form modified in the *Old English* and german text letters used by modren printers, and in the eclesiastical lettering used for inscriptions in churches. When the copyist had completed his work the manuscript was taken in hand by the designer, who skeched in the initial letter, ornamental borders, and pictures and handed it over to the iluminator, who painted in the coloring. The design and iluminating seem to have been really the most important feature in some of these early books and many splendid manuscripts, with there elabrate initials and delicate florishes and tracry spreading over the entire margins, are in existence still, reminders of an Art that existed once but now has passed away, perhaps forever.

ERNEST J. HATHAWAY, in THE INTERNATIONAL PRINTER, "THE INFLUENCE OF RELIGION IN EARLY BOOKMAKING."

Copyright, 1904,
by
Adèle Millicent Smith

Printed by
The John C. Winston Co.
Philadelphia

EXERCISES IN PROOFREADING
BY
ADÈLE MILLICENT SMITH

EXERCISE V—CORRECTED

EARLY PRINTING-PRESSES

The first printer had but small presses, made entirely of wood. Their power also was slight and they printed, as a rule, but one page a time. The screw was of wood, and worked by a bar," much the same as a modren napkin press. The chief thing was to obtain an even surface on the "bed" upon which the page of type rest; and, secondly, an even surface for the "Platen," which was lowered as the bar turned the screw, and thus pressed the paper upon the face of the type. The evenness of impression, as well as colour in many old books, show that this was acomplished with grate success, and proves what good mecanicians they were fore hundred years ago. It is a task whih we could not accomplish so successfully were our modern tools and apliances withdrawn.

* * * * * * * * * * * * * * *

There was nearly always two workmen to one press. One "beat" the "Form," that is, he dabbed two big soft balls covered with ink all over the type; the other placed the white paper on the "tympan," and ran the hole, by means of a whinch, beneath the *platen*, and then made a strong pull at the bar.

THE PENTATEUCH OF Printing: Blades

Copyright, 1904,
by
Adèle Millicent Smith

Printed by
The John C. Winston Co.
Philadelphia

EXERCISES IN PROOFREADING
BY
ADÈLE MILLICENT SMITH

EXERCISE VI—CORRECTED

NEWSPAPER PRINTING

The paper from which newspapers are printed is made in very long webs or rolls, varying in length from three to ninety miles, and prepared at special mills. A roll of paper is placed at one end of the press, above the floor, and the end of the sheet is then led between the cylinders. The paper, which enters the press simply as a blank roll, flies swiftly from cylinder to cylinder, receiving the impression of stereotypes, electrotypes, and half-tones, separates in newspapers under the action of the knife, divides again into sections, and issues form the press in the form of the finished newspaper, neatly folded and counted, ready for delivery.

The first journal in America appeared in Boston on September 25th, 1690, under the name Public Occurrences. This was a pamphlet, rather than a newspaper. The Boston *News-Letter* was started in 1704. The Boston Gazette appeared on December 21, 1719, and the American Weekly Mercury of Philadelphia, one day later. The Pennsylvania *Gazette* of philadelphia was started in 1728 by Samuel Keimer, but in less than a year it was bought by Benjamin Franklin. In 1821, it took the name of *The* Saturday Evening *Post:* under this title it is still issued, and is the *oldest* existing journal in America.

Copyright, 1904,
by
Adèle Millicent Smith

Printed by
The John C. Winston Co.
Philadelphia

EXERCISES IN PROOFREADING
BY
ADÈLE MILLICENT SMITH

EXERCISE VII—CORRECTED

THE INVENTION OF TYPOGRAPHY

The key to the invention of Typography was the typemould. The honor is due to the men who invented the first type-mold, for types which are *cast* are the ones only that can be used to advantage. A fierce controversy has waged as to who first gave the world a knowlege of typography, but the weight of evidence is strongly in favor of John Gutenberg, a printer of Mainz. We do not know when or were Gutenberg made his 1st experiments with movable type, but before 1450 he seems at Strasburg to have been at work endeavoring to perfect his art. From Strasburg he went to MainZ where his name appeared in 1448 in a record of a legal contract. Here about 1450, he enters into partnership with Johann means necessary to set up a printing-press. Fust or Faust, a wealthy moneylender, who furnished the In a few years (1455), Fust brought a law suit against Gutenberg to recover the sum money he had advanced. The verdict was in Fusts favor, and as Gutenberg could not pay the money, the printingpress passed out of his hands. Although now nearly old, sixty years Gutenberg did not despair, but determined to find another office. Some of his printing still materials remained to him, and the clerk of the town of Mainz provided him with mony. He continued to work for some time in Mainz. His death occurred about 1448.

Copyright, 1904,
by
Adèle Millicent Smith

Printed by
The John C. Winston Co.
Philadelphia

EXERCISES IN PROOFREADING
BY
ADÈLE MILLICENT SMITH

EXERCISE VIII—CORRECTED

EARLIEST PRINTED Works

The earliest specimen of printing from movable metal types known to exist at the present day is the famous *Letter* of Indulgence, of pope Nicholas V, to persons such as should contribute money to help the King of Cyprus against the Turks. A copy of this Indulgence, now preserved at the Hage, bears the earliest authentic date on a document printed from type, November 15, 1454.

The work upon which Gutenburg's fame rests as a great printer is the holy Bible in Latin. There are editions of this work one known as the Bible of Forty two Lines and the other as the Bible of *Thirty-six Lines*.

It is known not which printed first, but it is generally believed that the forty-two line Bible is earlier. It is beleved that this Bible could have been begun before August, 1450, and that it was finished in 1455, but the exact dates are not known. These editions of the Bible bear no printed date. The first book with a printed date is the Psalmorum codex of 1457, issued by Schœffer. This Palter is regarded by many as the finest works issued by the early press. It is an imtation not only of the copyists but of the iluminators art, with block stately types, and two colored Initials red and blue.

Copyright, 1904,
by
Adèle Millicent Smith

Printed by
The John C. Winston Co.
Philadelphia

EXERCISES IN PROOFREADING
BY
ADÈLE MILLICENT SMITH

EXERCISE IX—CORRECTED

MODERN PRESSWORK

In comparing the presswork of the sixteenth century with that of the close of the 19th, it would be satisfaction if we could not point to the same progress in the *quality* of work that we find in speed with which the work is executed. Unfortunately it must be admitted that that this is not uniformly the case. Not little satisfactory bookprinting is produced by the modern press but nevertheless it is the case that the demands made now upon the printer for books which can be sold at a poplar price has a tendency to bring fourth a quantity of presswork for which it is not possible to express admiration. It is with a feeling of great relief that one turns from some of the grey pages of the present ful old black-letter volumes of two or 3 centuries since, day, printed upon hard and stiff pulp paper, to the delight with their clearcut sharp type, struck with deep black ink on hand-made paper, of such stock as admitted not only of a perfect impression, but in addition, presented a surface and a flexibility delightful to the eye and to to the the touch.

AUTHORS AND PUBLISHERS: G. H. P. AND J. B. P.

The numerous illustrations which gives life and add value to our books, magazines and newspapers, without their increasing greatly cost, have been brought in existence by the development of the relatively new art of Photo-engraving, which by 1880 was beginning to supplant the reproducing of woodcuts.

Reproductions of any picture or object in which there is a gradtion of color, is made by the half-tone process. Drawings or pictures consisting of single lines, that is without tones of color are produced by lineplates.

EXERCISES IN PROOFREADING
BY
ADÈLE MILLICENT SMITH

EXERCISE X—CORRECTED

THE ROMAN AND the ITALIC TYPES

In 1458, the King of France sent Nicholas Jenson to
Mianz to learn the new art. On his return to Paris he tried
to get sufficient mony to establish the press, but was not
sucessful and went to Italy. In Venice he became famous.
Jonson prefected the roman type, which he used in 1471,
but the latter had already been cast at Subaco in 1465.
The roman letter of Jonson was a letter of extraordinary
beauty, it has freqently been copied, but never imitated.
Our roman letter of to-day is deried from the two scripts
formally used in Rome, capitals from the letters used from
insriptions, and small letters form the kursive form
employed for busness correspondence.

Aldus Manutius was an eminent printer, who lived in
Venice at the begining of the sixteenth century. He
he desired a compact type for the purpose of issuing small
editions of the classics, and to supply this need he introduced the type first knon as Venitian but called italic
afterward by the Latin and the English people. It is a
a letter wich inclines to the right, and is supposed to be formed
from the hand writing of Petrarch. The Aldine press established at Venice was celebrated for its editions of the greek
and and Latin classics. To assist him in the prepration of
these volumes, Aldus gathered around him, editors and
and proof readers, the most scolarly men of his age. The
present system of Punctuation may be said have been
devised by him, as but few marks before his time had
been employed, and the use of those was not well regulated

Copyright, 1904,
by
Adèle Millicent Smith

Printed by
The John C. Winston Co.
Philadelphia

EXERCISE XI—CORRECTED

THE GOTHIC LETTER

The book, issued by the first printers were in the Gothic characters. When the new art was introduced first the wealthy looked upon the inovation as an artistic trade, and the printers copied therefore the characters of of the cotemporary manuscript, in order to sell there works. The gothic letters had been employed by the copyists of Europe for many centuries before the invenvention of movable types. Roman type was first cast in 1465 by two German printers, Sweinhem and Panartz, at Subiaco, Italy. It was afterward prefected and used by Nicholas Jensen, at Venice. The gothic and the Roman fioms strugled together for some time after the interduction of printing, but the letter finally triumpfed. Roman type was used first in England in 1518, and by by the year 1800 books were printed generally in in that type. The roman letter of Jenson was the modle adopted by William Morris for the Kelmscott press, when it was started at Hammersmith, England, in 1891.

Although in printed work gothic characters proceded the roman, the letter had been emploied in manuscript, many centuries before the introduction of gothic letters. Gothic letter in fact was formed from the roman.

The English name of *black letter* was given to the caracter until after the introduction of roman printing types. Old English and German text are called by printers black letters.

Copyright, 1904,
by
Adèle Millicent Smith

Printed by
The John C. Winston Co.
Philadelphia

EXERCISES IN PROOFREADING
BY
ADÈLE MILLICENT SMITH

EXERCISE XII—CORRECTED

WILLIAM CAXTON

William Caxton is the first printer who practiced the Art in England. The year of his birth is not definitely known, but it was probably near 1422, for he was aprenticed in 1438 to the mercers trade. A few years after the latter date he left England for the Low Countries, where he remained for 30 years. About 1470 he entered the service of Margret, Duchess of Burgundy and sister of Edward IV. Caxton had long been intrested in the romances of the day, and had translated some of them. Having finished and been rewarded for his trouble in translating Le Recueil des Histoires de Troyes, for the duchess of Burgundy, he found his books in great demand. The English Nobles at Bruges wished to have copies of the favorite romances of the Age, and Caxton found himself able to supply the demand with sufficient rapidty. This brings us to the year 1472 or 1473. Mansoin, who had obtained some knowlege of art of printing, although certainly not from Colone, had just begun his typographical labors at Brugs, and was ready to reproduce copies by means of the press, if supported by the necesary patronage and funds. Caxton found the money, and Mansion the requisite knowledge, by the aid of wich appeared "The Recuyell," the book first printed in the English language. This, probably was not accomplished till 1474, and was succeeded, on Caxtons part, in another yea, by an issue of the Chess Book.

Copyright, 1904.
by
Adèle Millicent Smith

Printed by
The John C. Winston Co.
Philadelphia

EXERCISES IN PROOFREADING
BY
ADÈLE MILLICENT SMITH

EXERCISE XIII—CORRECTED

PRINTING IN CHINA and JAPAN

In China, various attempts have been made to substitute type for engraved blocks, but this is difficult because of the great number of the Chinese characters. These caracters do not stand for letters or sounds, but represent complete words or ideas, the characters formed by combination have been variously estimated, from two thousand to over two hundred thousand in number; not more than forteen or fifteen thousand, however, are in reglar use. A Chinese Missionary house employs about six thousand characters for an ordinary newspaper, only about four thousand are necessary; while magazines which treat of a great range of subjects, require ten thousand. The printing offices arrange the characters by the radicles. Movable types both of wood and of metal, have been employed long in China. Printing from movabel metal types are practised in China mainly for the purpose of circulating the Bible and the newspapers.

It is indisputable that block-printing was first practiced in China, but there is nothing which prove that Europe originally derived her knowledge of this art from the east.

In Japan, the earliest example of block printing dates from the midle of the eighth century. Because of the avidity with which the Japanese have took hold of western learning, printing is extensively carried on in Japan, both blocks and types of metal being employed.

Copyright 1904,
by
Adèle Millicent Smith

Printed by
The John C. Winston Co.
Philadelphia

EXERCISES IN PROOFREADING

BY

ADÈLE MILLICENT SMITH

EXERCISE XIV—CORRECTED

BEGINNING OF PRINTING IN AMERICA

In America printing began in the City of Mexico. The first printer was Juan Pablos, and the first book printed was "La Escala Espiritual para Llegar al Cielo" (A Spiritual Ladder for Reaching Heaven of San Juan Climaco, issued about 1536. So far as known, no copy of this book exists now. A press was established at Lima, Peru, about 1584. The first printing press in North America was erected at Cambridge, Massachusets, through the efforts of the Rev. Joss or Jesse Glover, who died while bringing the materials to that place. Glovers wife married Henry Dunster, the President of Harvard College, and he resumed the management of the Press. It was operated by Stephen Day, a workman who sailed with Glover. In 1639 it issued "The Freeman's Oath" and an almanac. Its first important work was "The Bay Psalm Book," printed in 1640.

Printing was begun in 1676 in Boston by John Foster. The first press in Philadelphia was set by William Bradford and the first work issued by him was an almanac in 1685. Bradford afterward moved to New York and began printing in that city in 1693.

Among the early books published in America, a few still retain their interest, for only not their quaintness but because of the influence they have exerted on the national character.

John Cotton's Catechism, or "Milk for Babies," first issued in England, was reprinted at Cambridge, Massachussetts, in 1656. This Catechism was afterwards included in another famous book, "The New England Primer," the first edition of which is supposed to have appeared between 1687 and 1690. The feature which must have made the Primer popular with children was its illustrations, especialy the rymed alphabet cuts.

Copyright 1904,
by
Adèle Millicent Smith

Printed by
The John C. Winston Co.
Philadelphia

EXERCISES IN PROOFREADING
BY
ADÈLE MILLICENT SMITH

EXERCISE XV—CORRECTED

BENJAMIN FRANKLIN

Benjamin Franklin was born in Boston on the 17 of January, 1706, and died in Philadelphia, on the 17th of April, 1790. He began his apprenticeship as a printer in 1718, and worked as a journeyman in Philadelphia in 1724, and in London in 1725. He returned to Philadelphia in 1726, and began as master printer in 1729. As editor and publisher he made himself a man of note. He invented the Franklin stove in 1742; he proved the identity of lighting and electricity in 1752; he was made Clerk of the Assembly in 1736; postmaster of Philadelphia; representative of Pensylvania before the Council of England in 1757 and again in 1764; delegate to Congress in 1775; ambassador to France in 1776; commissioner to England in 1783; President of Pennsylvania from 1785 to 1787; delegate to the Constitutional Convention in 1787.

THE PRACTICE OF TYPOGRAPHY:
Theodore Low DeVinne

In 1732 Franklin issued the first number of "Poor Richard's Almanac," which was published every year for a quarter of a century. "Poor Richard" made Franklin famous. He had noticed that in many homes this almanac was the only book. He therefor filled the space between the remarkable days in the calendar with proverbial sentences inculcating industry and frugality as the means of obtaining wealth and thereby (according to Franklin's belief) securing virtue; for he thought that the way to make people happy was to help them to be good. To the counsels of Poor Richard are due to some extent the shrewd, industrious and thrifty habits of the typical American.

RETURN TO ➡ **LIBRARY SCHOOL LIBRARY**
2 South Hall

642-2253

LOAN PERIOD 1	2	3
4	5	6

ALL BOOKS MAY BE RECALLED AFTER 7 DAYS

DUE AS STAMPED BELOW

SEP 1 8 1979		
DEC 1 9 1989		

FORM NO. DD 18, 45m, 6'76

UNIVERSITY OF CALIFORNIA, BERKELEY
BERKELEY, CA 94720

LD 21–100m-8,'34

www.ingramcontent.com/pod-product-compliance
Lightning Source LLC
Chambersburg PA
CBHW061037050726

47592CB00004B/1489